Original title:
The Search for Purpose in All the Wrong Places

Copyright © 2025 Creative Arts Management OÜ
All rights reserved.

Author: Henry Beaumont
ISBN HARDBACK: 978-1-80566-129-0
ISBN PAPERBACK: 978-1-80566-424-6

Signals from Distant Shores

I wandered far to find my aim,
Through beaches bright, I played a game.
I chased a crab and lost my shoe,
But oh, the sea's bright shades were true.

I asked a gull where dreams might lay,
It shrugged its wings and flew away.
A fish, confused, just blinked at me,
I laughed aloud - it felt so free.

With every wave, I sought a sign,
But all I found was salty brine.
A treasure map showed "X" too late,
But hey, I found my lunch plate fate.

So here's my tale of quests gone wrong,
With laughter mixed in my own song.
Next time I plan to find my goal,
I'll bring a map, and maybe a shoal.

The Scent of Forgotten Roads

I drove my car on roads unknown,
In search of sunshine, all alone.
I passed a llama, wearing shades,
It winked at me—how dreams cascade!

A map I followed, full of holes,
But ended at some garden shoals.
I found a cat with wisdom deep,
It gave advice in feline leaps.

Through winding paths of fragrant pines,
I thought I'd find some grand designs.
Yet only found a pizza place,
Where crusts made history with each face.

So here's my lesson on this quest,
Sometimes the way is not the best.
With laughter shared, I'll roam again,
And maybe find a better friend.

Serenity on a Stormy Sea

A sailor dreams of sunny climes,
But finds himself on waves that chime.
He casts his net for fish divine,
Yet only pulls up shoes and wine.

With seagulls laughing at his plight,
He wonders where he went so slight.
In storms he thinks he's had enough,
But finds the wet is kind of tough.

Reflections in a Shattered Mirror

Peering at a cracked facade,
He sees his face, a funny charade.
Each shard reflects a different tale,
Like socks that always seem to fail.

He fixes hair with utmost care,
While tripping on a chair somewhere.
His inner clown makes quite the scene,
With dreams more ridiculous than they seem.

Yearning for What Was Never There

He longs for spells that lost their gleam,
And chases shadows in a dream.
With every twist of fate's cruel hand,
He seeks the truth in a magic band.

A rabbit's foot and luck unplanned,
His wishes float like grains of sand.
In every joke, he seeks the clue,
Just to find he'd rather chew a shoe.

Mermaids in the Desert

Amidst the dunes, they sing and sway,
Mermaids lost, think they're on a bay.
They brush the sand with scales of grace,
While wondering where the fishy place.

With sunscreen slathered on their tails,
They float on dreams, but not on gales.
In search of water, they just grin,
Their laughter echoes, a wild spin.

Digging for Gold in Dust

With a shovel in hand, I dig with great zest,
Hoping to find treasures where dirt likes to rest.
My neighbors just giggle and roll their eyes wide,
As I keep unearthing the trash I can't hide.

A shiny old bottle, a tin can thrown far,
I pause and I ponder, is this a gold star?
But alas, it's just trash with a glimmer of rust,
Where dreams of great riches melt down to mere dust.

Maps Made of Clouds

I bought a fine map, drawn on clouds in the breeze,
They promised me treasures beneath shady trees.
With each sunny step, I trip on a fact,
That clouds don't hold treasures, they simply just act.

I follow the shapes and I dance to the sounds,
But unicorns scatter on fluffy white grounds.
My compass keeps spinning, lost in the air,
No riches or fortune, just blows through my hair.

The Siren Call of Solitude

In quietness I sat, with silence my friend,
Expecting deep answers from thoughts that won't end.
But solitude giggled and whispered aloud,
'Your mind is a circus, come join the big crowd!'

I searched for enlightenment, found nothing but jest,
As my thoughts danced around like a jester's quest.
So I called up my buddies, oh what a delight,
Turns out the loudness was clearer than night.

Truths Buried Beneath Lies

They said, 'Dig deep!' like a mole in the soil,
But every truth found was wrapped up in foil.
I unwrapped the layers, one laugh at a time,
To find that the truth had a knack for slapstick mime.

I laughed at the notion, I chuckled in glee,
As fibs turned to jokes, like bad comedy.
So I shrug off the dig for the hidden surprise,
Guess truths need their jokes to wear silly disguise.

Lost Among the Stars

I aimed my rocket high, oh yes,
To find my joy in cosmic mess.
But floating past a taco stand,
I lost my map, now isn't that grand!

The Milky Way just spilled its milk,
While comets dashed like threads of silk.
I searched for meaning in the void,
Found only snacks, completely devoid!

Satellites dance, but what's the song?
A playlist that feels all too wrong.
Asteroids crash like dreams unmet,
Yet here I am, not done just yet!

I guess I'll lounge on Mars instead,
With interstellar thoughts in my head.
I'll trade my rocket for a seat,
And laugh at my own cosmic defeat!

The Mirage of Fulfillment

I wandered into shops of dreams,
Where nothing's ever what it seems.
Each glittered item's just a lie,
Like buying wings, but I can't fly.

This potion claimed to bring me bliss,
Yet all it did was leave a hiss.
With every goal I thought I'd find,
Came selfie sticks to cloud my mind.

The shiny things just lead to woes,
Another round of 'who really knows?'
I bought a map, it showed me wrong,
"Just follow your heart" – that felt strong!

Now trapped inside a virtual maze,
Trading real life for endless plays.
I raise a toast with all my friends,
To searching hard, but what just ends!

Sifting Through Ashes of Dreams

I checked my closet for an idea,
Found yesterday's hopes, oh dear, oh dear!
Each pair of shoes a journey gone,
Still, here I sit, no plans to don.

I sifted through the dust of chance,
To locate hope amid the prance.
But what I found was just a sock,
A mismatched pair with a dull rock!

I thought of building up a throne,
Out of things I used to own.
But ashes only make great mess,
And fire alarms need to address!

So here I am, holding a spatula,
To cook up dreams as if I'd ratula.
With laughter bubbling from the stove,
I find my purpose, in leftovers I rove!

A Compass Without Direction

I bought a compass, it just spins,
Turns out it's good for party wins.
It points at places I can't find,
Like happiness or peace of mind.

I'm lost in woods of expectations,
Chasing squirrels with wild elations.
"Just follow your heart" the slogan screams,
But my heart's busy with other schemes.

Trekking paths that lead to snacks,
Dodging pitfalls, tax, and hacks.
Yet every turn's a different plight,
Then I trip over my own plight!

So raise a toast with laughter's cheer,
To navigating life, we must veer.
A compass may not know the beat,
But who needs maps when joy's the treat?

Echoes of Lost Trails

In the cupboard, snacks are hid,
I thought I'd find my peace amid.
But crumbs and crumbs, not quite the grace,
Just mouse tracks in a hungry race.

I searched the fridge, oh what a sight,
Leftover pizza from last night.
Instead of dreams, I found a scheme,
To live my life on cheesy cream.

I wandered through the park so green,
Tossed a coin, you know the scene.
Made a wish for something grand,
But all I got was ice cream in hand.

So here I am, with toast and jam,
Chasing purpose, where's the plan?
In every bite and every laugh,
I find my solace on this path.

Seeking Solace in Silhouettes

I chased my goals in weird cafes,
Thought fortune hid in frothy bays.
But cappuccinos make me frown,
As baristas spin the world around.

I tried the gym, but oh so tough,
The treadmill makes me feel so gruff.
I thought I'd run towards the light,
But stumbled, spilt my drink—what a sight!

I signed up for a clever class,
They taught me how to write alas.
But all I penned was doodles bold,
My purpose lost, my dreams on hold.

So here I sit, with pen in hand,
Chasing dreams that slip like sand.
In every laugh, in every jest,
I find that maybe fun's the best.

When Dreams Wander Astray

I sought the stars from my backyard,
But found instead a grumpy bard.
He said to me, with graying hair,
Dreams are just dreams, go shed a tear.

Explored the world of online fame,
Joined a workshop, what a game!
But all I learned was how to pose,
While my pet cat just stole the shows.

I lurked in shadows, scouting heights,
Thinking I'd find some wise insights.
But tripped on shoes, that weren't my size,
Turns out my dreams were in disguise.

With laughter ringing, I'll confess,
Purpose is tricky, I must address.
In every stumble, every sway,
I find my joy, come what may!

Heartbeats in Distant Cities

I booked a trip to distant lands,
But forgot to pack my silly plans.
In every port, I lost my way,
Chasing taxis that won't obey.

I questioned maps, I flipped and turned,
For wisdom, coffee I keenly yearned.
Yet every cup just brewed more doubt,
What's this purpose that I'm about?

I danced with strangers, told them tales,
Hoping my heart would share the trails.
Yet all they did was wink and run,
Leaving me chasing after fun.

So here's to cities, bright and loud,
With every heartbeat, I'm so proud.
In laughter's echo, let me roam,
For in the joy, I've found my home.

Whirlwinds of Uncertainty

In a hat shop, lost my mind,
Looking for purpose, none to find.
A rabbit popped out, said with glee,
"You'll need a map to find the knee!"

Spinning 'round in a lifetime's chase,
Found my joy in a shoe's embrace.
Danced with penguins, why not, you say?
When in doubt, wear socks all day!

Chasing rainbows on a pogo stick,
Every bounce, a new little trick.
Fruits of labor fell from the trees,
I stumbled right into a bee's Jamboree!

Cupcakes and dreams held as my guide,
Bumping into the pie I tried to hide.
In search of meaning, I found delight,
In frosting whispers in every bite.

Pilgrimages to Forgotten Places

Off to find gold, or perhaps just cheese,
In a cave that smelled oddly of peas.
With a map drawn by a squirrel in haste,
I realized I wasn't leaving this place!

Each open door, a game of chance,
Could lead to wisdom or a silly dance.
A relic sought, the prize of the quest,
Was an old sock—hey, it's still the best!

Met a wise owl, who wore a bow tie,
Said, "Purpose is a pizza, that's no lie!"
You take a slice, but mind the crust,
For lost in cheese is where we trust!

Through dusty lanes and under old skies,
I collected stories, not just goodbyes.
In every detour, a laugh I'd lace,
Turns out my trip was just a big race!

A Tangle of Unfinished Tales

A book unopened, filled with dust,
Pages of dreams turned into rust.
But as I flipped, the words flew wild,
A cat in the story, oh, what a child!

Characters fled, but I followed fast,
Each one a mystery, spun unsurpassed.
A knight without armor, a dragon who teases,
Said, "Join my quest for the world's lost cheeses!"

Wrote a letter to a time-traveling frog,
In hopes he'd send back a witty monologue.
Instead, he sent me a loaf of bread,
"For adventures, dear friend, you must be fed!"

The tales are tangled, like hair after swimming,
But laughter and joy have me still grinning.
Each ended chapter, a new start in store,
In this book of nonsense, who could ask for more?

The Art of Lost Adventures

I set out for glory, just me and my snack,
Ended up sitting on a very wide track.
The sunset was lovely, the journey divine,
Until a raccoon stole my pizza slice, oh, fine!

Wrote my regrets on napkins and leaves,
Spoke to the moon as it giggled and weaves.
In a circus of thoughts, I tumbled right in,
Trained by the clowns—hey, it's quite the win!

With a compass that points to a donut shop,
I wandered through fields, with each hearty plop.
Found a treasure chest filled with confetti,
Turns out, the map led me to a spaghetti!

So here's to the missteps, the laughter and mess,
Each blunder a blessing, I must confess.
With every lost adventure that comes my way,
I find the best joy in each silly day!

Whispers in Empty Corridors

In halls where echoes play and roam,
I chase the laughter, feel at home.
A mirror laughs, it can't be true,
I swear it just spilled coffee too.

With each step forward, I trip on air,
As shoes and dreams become a pair.
The walls keep whispering silly things,
Like how to dance without two wings.

Fumbling thoughts like socks in dryers,
Burning questions like misplaced pliers.
I ask the plants about my fate,
They shrug their leaves, they just can't wait.

So here I wander, lost yet bold,
In this quaint circus of my own fold.
With every misstep, I wear a grin,
Embracing chaos, where fun begins.

The Labyrinth of Longing

In mazes where the cheese is fake,
I stroll in circles, for goodness' sake.
Each turn a mix of hope and jest,
Where squirrels laugh at my quest for the best.

I find a sign that says, "Turn left!"
It also says, "This path's a theft."
My sense of direction's lost in a spin,
Like a cat that forgot how to win.

Amidst the hedges growing quite wide,
I seek the meaning, my trusty guide.
The gnomes are gossiping by the pond,
Their wisdom, alas, a little beyond.

Yet in this twisty route of laughter,
I spot a frog dressed as a pastor.
He croaks a tune, it calls to me,
"Adventure's fun, just wait and see!"

Pursuit of Forgotten Paths

Along the routes where lost shoes lay,
I wander aimless, day by day.
Each corner turned, a new surprise,
As pigeons plot my next disguise.

A fork in the road looks like a tease,
One way is chaos, the other, fleas.
I toss a coin and hear it land,
Right on a lady's ice cream stand.

With every step, I collect small quirks,
Like sticky notes where nonsense lurks.
The trees giggle as I pass them by,
With owls that wink and butterflies fly.

But in this chase of whims and glee,
I find the joy of being free.
I'll skip and hop, take life's parade,
In paths forgotten, memories made.

When Hopes Drift Like Leaves

In autumn skies where hopes descend,
I chase the gusts that twist and bend.
Leaves swirl like thoughts, lost in the breeze,
With every flutter, my mind's at ease.

A wish once planted, now stuck in tree,
With branches waving, come dance with me.
I trip on dreams while skipping stones,
And laugh at fate with hats and phones.

Each tumble down, a chuckle shared,
As gravity plays, underscored and bared.
A ladybug offers me advice,
"Just follow the wind, it's never precise!"

So here I drift on whims, bemused,
Wrapped in laughter, slightly confused.
For as leaves fall, my chuckles grow,
In this wild chase, I'm the star of the show.

Frayed Edges of Lost Intentions

I wandered down a noodle shop,
In hopes my life would stir and hop.
Instead, I found a soggy fate,
With fortune cookies on my plate.

I tried my luck at fishing lines,
Surely wisdom in the brines.
Yet all I caught was old shoe laces,
With hints of all my thought displaces.

Through aisles of socks and broken dreams,
I sought the truth in darning seams.
But all I found was mismatched pairs,
And laughter echoing through my cares.

So here I stand with a jumbled grin,
Sipping tea beneath the din.
In every mishap, life's a jest,
In tangled threads, I seek my best.

Vagrancy of the Soul

I trekked along the city streets,
In search of answers, maybe beats.
I asked a pigeon, wise and old,
It cooed, "Just eat; be brave, be bold!"

I crashed a party of lost socks,
Got tipsy on mismatched clocks.
Each tick-tock whispered, "Chill out mate,
Life's just a dance; don't contemplate!"

With a hat of daisies on my head,
I sought the wisdom from the bread.
Yet all it gave was crumbs and fluff,
And laughter that was quite enough.

Now I giggle with my wandering heart,
In zany journeys, I find my part.
For in the chaos, I reclaim my role,
As the glorious vagrant of my soul.

Starlit Pathways to Nowhere

I tried to trace the stars at night,
Hoping they'd guide me with their light.
But I stumbled on a garden gnome,
Who offered me a ride back home.

"Follow the trails," the moonlight said,
But I got lost in a field of dread.
With fireflies making quite the show,
I ended up at the neighbor's hoe.

I chased my dreams on roller skates,
And whirlwind winds with silly fates.
But turns out I was only back,
Where ducks quacked loud, in nature's hack.

So here I laugh under the stars,
As silly wishes fall like cars.
For pathways twist and turn with ease,
And nowhere leads to all my cheese.

Reaching for Stars Behind the Clouds

I climbed a tree, thought I'd reach heights,
To grasp the stars through fiber lights.
But all I found were squirrels tattle,
And acorns starting a weird rattle.

With a shiny lollipop in hand,
I sought the secrets of this land.
To fly with dreams as big as boulders,
But all I got were soggy shoulders.

Tried flipping pancakes in the sky,
Hoping they'd float and maybe fly.
But they just flopped with syrup drips,
While birds collected the tasty bits.

Yet still I stretch for those bright things,
With a dance and rash of silly swings.
For behind those clouds lies a jest,
And life's best pleasures are like a quest.

Lost in the Labyrinth of Longing

Once I chased my dreams with glee,
But tripped on shoelaces, oh me!
I asked a squirrel for advice,
It said, 'Your snacks, just roll the dice!'

I wandered through a maze of trees,
Where even lost socks found some keys.
The compass spun like a disco ball,
As I followed the dog's friendly call.

Maps made of jelly just won't do,
I tried to read clouds; they just turned blue.
I found a sign that said 'Go Left!'
But my navigation skills are bereft.

In circles I dance, what a fine plight,
Searching for meaning in a chocolate fight.
With every bite, my purpose fades,
Yet laughter echoes in life's charades.

Notes from the Edge of Nothing

I scribble thoughts on napkins worn,
While contemplating a world so torn.
My pen runs dry, and so does my wit,
I guess that's life—a comedy skit.

The edges of nothing, a fine circus,
With juggling acts of dreams that surface.
I tried to catch clouds with fishing hooks,
Discovering joy in the strangest nooks.

A voice from nowhere echoes my fears,
It's just the cat, giving me cheers.
I tiptoe through life's wild amusement,
In this grand jest, I find my alignment.

The punchlines buried under my bed,
Each missed cue leads to more dread.
Yet laughter's the treasure, pure and bright,
And I'll keep roaming till the morning light.

Fleeting Hopes on Untrodden Roads

I strolled down roads that weren't quite there,
Tripped over hopes like fresh air.
Each step taken, a dance with fate,
I met a goose who wouldn't wait.

I wondered if detours made sense,
Or if life's just a funny suspense.
A lollipop tree whispered my fate,
'Sometimes, just laugh; don't contemplate!'

With every mile, I lost my way,
Yet found a dog, wanted to play.
His wagging tail, my true north star,
In this quirky journey, I'll go far.

So here's to roads that lead us astray,
They often bring laughter along the way.
With fleeting hopes and silly dreams,
Life's a joke—it bursts at the seams.

Searching for Stars Beneath the Sea

Why search for stars in the night sky,
When dolphins dance and seagulls fly?
I dove deep where the seaweed sways,
Found lost beach toys from bygone days.

The ocean's twist, a playful prank,
Gave me fish that swam in a tank.
They spoke of worlds, both wild and odd,
But left me floundering, feeling flawed.

With seashells whispering tales of glee,
I waded through dreams submerged in debris.
A crab wore shades, with style to test,
'No stars down here, but jesters are best!'

So here I float on a jellyfish dream,
In search of visions that sparkle and gleam.
With laughter my compass, I'm free as a bee,
Underwater wisdom, just let it be.

The Weight of Unfulfilled Dreams

I chased my dreams like a dog in a park,
But they slipped away, oh, what a lark.
I thought I had it, a plan all neat,
But ended up snoring, face down on my seat.

The brochure promised life in high gear,
Instead, I'm stuck wearing mismatched gear.
With every new venture, I levitate high,
Then land with a plop, with a pie in my eye.

I wear my regrets like a cozy old coat,
It's full of holes and smells like a goat.
Yet I laugh at the chaos, spin tales that amaze,
'This isn't a failure, just a comedic maze!'

So toss out the weight and embrace the light,
Let's dance on the failures and party all night.
For every odd turn brings a giggle, it's true,
Life's humor shines bright when dreams are askew.

Dandelions Dancing in the Wind

A dandelion wishes, it dreams of the sun,
With each little puff, it's losing the fun.
It spirals away like a runaway kite,
Chasing a breeze, what a comical sight.

I tried to catch fortune, just like that seed,
But tripped on my shoelace, I couldn't quite heed.
It scattered like laughter, went off in a swirl,
While I sat there snickering, a disheveled girl.

Grabbed by the whims of a gusty old gale,
I'm darting like dandelions, telling my tale.
'Oh look at me go!' I shouted, quite proud,
But landed in mud, oh, to my own crowd!

Yet amid the mishaps, I'll leap once again,
For life is a jig, even when filled with rain.
With each little tumble, I just can't resign,
I'll dance like the dandelions, wild and divine!

Moonlight on Untamed Seas

Under the moon, I set sail with a grin,
With a map made of ketchup, that's where I begin.
The stars were my guides, or so I believed,\nTurned out
they were just reflections, deceived.

I thought I'd find treasure, gold and grand loot,
Instead, I found seaweed and my old boot.
The waves laughed and tossed me, what a fine jig,
As I paddled with chopsticks, feeling so big.

But who needs a map when you can just drift?
With each slap of the wave, I get a new gift.
Tall tales of my voyage will fill every space,
Of pirates and mermaids, like a child's embrace.

So here's to the moon and her dance on the waves,
To mischief and laughter, the fun it engraves.
For purpose is silly when joy takes the lead,
And the world is a playground, not just a need.

Myths of Return and Discovery

I packed my bags for the journey ahead,
With snacks and a dream, I felt well-fed.
But maps led me in circles, round and round,
Found myself back where the snacks were found.

They said, 'Seek adventure, escape and explore,'
Yet all I discovered was my front door.
I traveled to places with names hard to say,
But returned to my couch, binge-watching all day.

With stories to tell of the gems that I found,
Like a pizza slice lost in a spacecraft sound.
Each mission a riot, with laughter and cheer,
For who needs a goal when you've got good beer?

So raise up your glass to the silly and bold,
Embrace every trip, even ones made of gold.
For myths of return are just jokes in disguise,
And laughter's the treasure that opens our eyes.

A Journey toward the Unknown

In a land where socks go to hide,
I seek my dreams, yet they subside.
Chasing tails of whimsical thoughts,
Finding answers in tangled knots.

With a map made of crumpled fries,
I trudge through mists of clouded skies.
Every corner, a laughing ghost,
Where hopes arrive but fears are toast.

The compass spins, oh what a sight,
Leading me to snacks, not insight.
I ponder deep, in a puddle of goo,
As rubber ducks bid me adieu.

Yet amidst the chaos and the cheer,
I stumble upon a truth so clear.
Splashing in puddles, I find my joy,
Not in maps, but in each little toy.

Where Promises Meet Disillusionment

I signed a pact with a chocolate cake,
Promised love, but it made me ache.
It vanished quick, a sweet delight,
Leaving crumbs and a sad bite.

The fortune cookie said to strive,
Yet I just sat, with no drive.
Hoping for wisdom, I cracked it wide,
Said 'Eat more cake,' then took a ride.

I chased my thoughts down a plastic drain,
Looked for answers, but found only gain.
Each wrong turn, a twist of fate,
I laughed until I lost my plate.

With every promise that fades away,
I dance on bubble wrap, come what may.
Life has quirks, and that's the fun,
In a world of chaos, I'm never done.

The Allure of Fleeting Echoes

Whispers in the wind, like cats in hats,
I chase the echoes of my thoughts like rats.
Each fleeting moment, a jig and a zap,
Where giggles linger and silly maps.

"Look over here!" the echoes tease,
Leading me deeper with laugh and wheeze.
Like fireflies that flicker in the night,
Dancing just out of reach, oh what a sight!

I ask a shadow the meaning of life,
It winks at me, then scurries with strife.
I dig through confetti, but find no clue,
Just sprinkles of laughter and some goo.

Yet in the chaos, I sip my drink,
Cheers to moments that make me think.
For in the laughter, I find my grace,
Chasing echoes leads to a funny place.

Reflections in the Stillness of Time

In the mirror, I see a curious face,
Trying to turn each frown into race.
Gazing at wrinkles like rows of delight,
Time's silly dance, a whimsical flight.

I ponder my past, then burst into song,
Why do I worry? I've been here so long!
With each wink of the clock, I laugh out loud,
At the silly antics of my own proud crowd.

What is my purpose? The cat just yawns,
As I twirl around like a dancer with prawns.
Life's but a jest, a bubble of fun,
Filled with moments to savor, each one!

And as the hours slip by like a breeze,
I find my peace in a world full of cheese.
With giggles and snacks, I pass through the day,
For even in stillness, I dance my own way.

Riddles in the Starlit Skies

A cat in a hat seeks delight,
Counting the stars in the night,
Wishing on wishes that never came true,
Finding lost socks as a cosmic brew.

Dancing with mice in the moon's glow,
Chasing their tails, oh what a show!
Turning around, they forgot the fun,
Did they ever know that they'd missed the sun?

Beyond the Horizon's Grasp

She sold her compass for a shiny pearl,
Thinking it'd guide her through the whirl,
But when she opened it, what did she find?
A map to nowhere, oh what a grind!

With socks on her hands, she danced with glee,
Peddling her moments, carefree as can be,
Yet as she pranced, her shoes fell apart,
Maybe the lost were where she should start!

Unseen Vistas of Being

Bouncing with bubbles, a ball of fluff,
Claiming the world can never be tough,
But beneath the laughter, a tickle of doubt,
Where's the exit on this goofy route?

Out in the garden where weeds wear crowns,
Searching for wisdom in silly towns,
Each twist and tumble – a lesson disguised,
While squirrels debated who's the most wise!

A Glimmer in the Mist

Lost in the fog, sat a wise old goat,
With jokes that he told on a half-sunk boat,
Asking for answers from fish with no shoes,
They only said, 'What's there left to lose?'

He chuckled and chewed on his favorite grass,
Filling the air with a smelly sass,
Yet in the mucky, murky delight,
Sometimes the answers blind in plain sight!

The Illusion of Perfect Destinations

I hiked the mountain, oh so tall,
With visions grand, I aimed for a fall.
But the top was just a snack bar's scene,
And my quest for glory felt kinda mean.

I jumped on a train, thought I'd find my bliss,
But it took me in circles, oh what a miss!
The ticket said 'dream,' but I got a nap,
Now my goals are just a silent clap.

In search of a job that would light my fire,
I found a gig as a laundry dryer.
With fabric softener dreams, oh what a twist,
I'm clean but unsatisfied, that's the gist.

So here I sit, with snacks in hand,
Laughing at maps that don't understand.
If life's a journey, I'm just in the way,
Chasing train wrecks and buffet trays.

Navigating Through a Fog of Questions

Woke up one morning, my mind in a whirl,
Expected enlightenment, but just found a swirl.
Thought I'd find answers in the cereal box,
But all I got was sugar and some strange rocks.

I asked a goldfish for wisdom on life,
He just swam in circles, avoiding my strife.
"Fish, can you guide me?" I did implore,
He blinked back at me, then hid under the floor.

I took to the sky, in search of my fate,
But all I found was a bird on a plate.
"Where do I go?" I yelled to the breeze,
It just giggled and blew through the trees.

Putting my faith in fortune cookies,
Got a fortune full of weird looking rookies.
So here I ponder, with questions galore,
Navigating the fog, unsure of the score.

Tangled Threads of Ambition

I tried to knit my life into a quilt,
But the yarn just tangled with ambition built.
A scarf for success turned into a mess,
I wore it with pride; it's my new dress.

I climbed the ladder, step by step,
But my shoelace caught, oh what a rep!
Now I'm dangling here, in a knot of my dreams,
Screaming for help while my vision deems.

In search of a career, I took off my hat,
But my head was still spinning like a flying bat.
Thought I could sew up the perfect plan,
But ended up making a mismatched span.

So I weave my way through life's odd design,
With threads of laughter and a hint of whine.
If ambition's a tapestry, let's call it a spree,
With colors that clash—just like me!

Uncharted Waters of Desire

Set sail for passion in a leaky boat,
With maps made of wishes and a love for remote.
The compass spun round, never quite sure,
And the crew was a flock of birds that endure.

I dove for treasure, where gold should be,
But found only seaweed, quite crafty you see.
With dreams in my pocket and fish on my plate,
My fortune was slim, but my costs were great.

Drifting along on my ship made of hope,
I tried to fish out a new way to cope.
But all I caught was a rubbery shoe,
Tossed back to the sea, as I bid adieu.

So here I anchor, in the bay of odd wants,
With a heart full of giggles and whimsical taunts.
If desire's an ocean, I'm just a small wave,
Riding the ripples, forever a knave.

The Quest for a Fading Light

In the fridge I find a treasure,
Leftover cake from a week of leisure.
But with each slice, my dreams take flight,
Okay, maybe not, but it feels so right.

I chased the sun to the edge of town,
Only to see the clouds frown down.
Searching hard in the wrong direction,
I guess I'll settle for astral perfection.

With a map drawn on a napkin bright,
I wander through the bistro's twilight.
Finding nuggets of joy in each wrong turn,
Who knew ignorance was a way to learn?

Yet here I stand, with a grin so wide,
Knowing the journey's just a whimsical ride.
Sometimes we laugh, sometimes we sigh,
But who needs purpose when you can just fly?

Searching the Bottom of Broken Bottles

I peered into a bottle, cracked and grim,
Hoping to find wisdom on a whim.
But all I got was a cork and a laugh,
The secret to joy? Just follow the path!

Each sip of ale brings a new idea,
Was that a philosopher or just a beer?
I chuckle at thoughts that come from the haze,
Maybe my purpose is to drink on Fridays.

With each empty glass, my worries grow thin,
Or was it the beer making me spin?
Every bottom I check reveals a new twist,
Faced with the notion I've surely missed.

I stumble along, with a friend so dear,
We toast to the nothing, we toast to the here.
For what's life if not filled with glee?
Searching for answers, just let it be!

Footprints in Shifting Sands

I wrote my plans on the beach so fine,
But waves sneer back, 'This is not a line!'
Sandcastles crumble, dreams just like clay,
Maybe I'll find them in the dunes today.

My footprints dance like they know the move,
Yet each step forward is less of a groove.
Searching for meaning beneath the sun's glare,
Oh look, a seagull! Does it even care?

I skip and jump, feeling quite spry,
But the tide pulls me back, oh me, oh my!
A treasure map drawn with a stick in the sand,
Leads only to laughter, though it wasn't planned.

Footprints fade, but the joy stays bright,
Chasing sunsets with all of my might.
So here's to the wandering, the silly, the fun,
Sometimes the aimless is best when it's done!

Emptiness at the End of the Road

I drove all night searching high and low,
For meaning, for answers, or just a glow.
I finally arrived, but what did I find?
A closed café and a sign that's blind.

The map was a joke, ha! What a twist,
Where's my purpose? I've got the gist.
Maybe the journey has all been a sham,
But my pet rock is a great little ham!

So I laughed at the sign that claimed: 'This is it!'
Who knew the void could be such a hit?
I twirled in my seat and tossed my old goals,
Embracing the madness, life's just for souls!

With empty roads stretching far and wide,
I'll make the best of this unplanned ride.
For at the end of the road, I've gained a new friend,
And we'll laugh at the nothing until it's the end!

Tracing the Lines Between Us

I looked for meaning in my sock drawer,
Found only mismatched pairs galore.
Conversations hidden in a crumpled note,
But all I got was a pizza remote.

I wandered through life with jellybeans,
Trying to find what all this means.
Each color pops, but taste can't show,
Is life a circus? I'm not sure, though.

I asked my cat, who just stared,
And curled up tight, clearly unprepared.
Searching high, searching low,
Turns out my purpose's just for show.

With every step, I trip and fall,
Chasing shadows that aren't there at all.
Perhaps my calling is a fine dessert,
A slice of pie, with very little dirt.

The Pulse of the Unexplored

I sailed a boat made of old newspaper,
Hoping to rough it, like some wild caper.
Instead I found a soggy hat,
Who knew lost treasure was just a rat?

In search of wisdom, I climbed a tree,
Thought I'd find answers way up high, you see.
But all I found was a bird that squawked,
Sending me back where the ground had talked.

I crossed a bridge that led to nowhere,
With a sign that read, 'Beware of despair!'
But laughter echoed from beneath my feet,
Turns out the trolls were quite sweet to meet.

Wandering paths with mismatched shoes,
Contemplating life while sipping on blues.
If purpose hides in a chocolate bar,
Then I've found my goal, and it's not too far.

Chasing Rainbows on Sunless Days

I chased a rainbow, took off in a sprint,
Found only puddles and an old paint tint.
Each drop a reminder of dreams gone slack,
But the joy was in jumping, not just the track.

I searched for gold at the end of the hue,
Met a leprechaun who offered some stew.
Said, 'Follow my lead, and you'll surely find,
The best treasure is laughter, and joy intertwined.'

The clouds rumbled laughter, quite out of place,
'We've been here forever, just slowing the race.'
Chasing reflections that shift and sway,
Turns out my journey's just wild and play.

With each silly twist, I'm learning to grin,
That purpose may just be where the fun begins.
Sunless days shine with a spirit that thrills,
I'll chase the odd colors and see what it spills!

Where Seasons Meet and Fade

In spring, I planted seeds of doubt,
Watered with laughter, let joy sprout.
But the flowers were all made of cheese,
And the rabbits laughed, 'Do what you please!'

Summer brought sunshine and a wild dance,
But I tripped on grass that didn't give a chance.
With every awkward move and silly spin,
I pondered if wisdom was really a win.

Autumn rolled in with a shifty breeze,
Leaves turned to gold, but I sneezed with ease.
Each leaf had a tale, all woven in time,
But they rustled away, like a half-baked rhyme.

Finally, winter wrapped me in white,
With snowflakes whispering, 'You're alright.'
I learned the seasons, though wild and grand,
Are best explored with a funny little hand.

Maps Unfolded in Despair

I took a map to the grocery store,
But it led me to the candy floor.
Chocolate mountains and soda streams,
I meant to shop, but now I'm lost in dreams.

A compass spinning, what could it mean?
Found a sandwich that looked like a queen.
In every aisle, a new twist of fate,
My endless quest for a proper plate.

I stumbled on cookies shaped like stars,
Promised this journey would take me far.
Instead, I'm stuck in snack attack,
With no way to find my way back.

Maps and snacks conspire and play,
Purpose has fled, swept out with the tray.
Laughter takes hold of my weary mind;
In this candy kingdom, what will I find?

Chasing Reflections in Glass

I chased my reflection in a shop's front pane,
It winked back at me, driving me insane.
Tried to connect, but it just grinned,
Mimicking my moves like a long-lost twin.

A shadow danced, wearing a silly hat,
We jived and jiggled, a whimsical spat.
Through every window, I sought a guide,
But all I found was a goofy ride.

Where's the wisdom, the grand design?
Just me and my shadow, sipping on wine.
Together we laughed at life's little gaps,
Purpose eludes us while we plot our naps.

In a mirror maze, I called out for fate,
Only echoes returned; isn't that great?
Chasing reflections, I lost all the clues,
But gained a good laugh, that's something to use!

The Mirage of Meaning

Out in the desert, I searched for truth,
But found a cactus wearing a tooth.
It smiled wide, said, 'Look around!'
Meaning's a mirage, lost and found.

I wandered far, chasing a dream,
Only to trip on a buttercream stream.
A cake that sings and a pie that dances,
What a place to take my chances!

Here I was thinking I'd find my way,
Stumbling on desserts that begged me to play.
If purpose is pastry, I'm rolling in dough,
Just not the kind that helps me to grow.

So bring me laughter, and I'll forget the map,
With sugary moments, there's no time to nap.
In a world of sweetness, I'm free to explore,
Perhaps the meaning was laughter, not more!

Footprints on Unworn Paths

I ventured forth on a path less trod,
Found lost shoes that belonged to a pod.
Footprints zigzag, quite out of place,
Led to a garden with a croissant grace.

I picked up a shoe, it sparkled delight,
Next to a spoon, how strange is that sight?
An uncolored world filled with flavors and flair,
Each odd discovery takes me somewhere rare.

In a land where marmalade rivers flow,
I questioned my journey, where should I go?
But laughter erupted, as jam became gold,
And the more I wandered, the less I felt old.

With sassy footprints that knew no end,
I chuckled and danced, made an odd new friend.
In unworn paths, where nonsense thrives,
Maybe purpose is fun, where laughter derives!

Finding Fireflies in the Day

In daylight, I hunt for those lights,
Chasing sparks that hide from sights.
My net is made from an old pizza box,
Yet all I catch are confused knocks.

My friends just laugh, they don't understand,
Why I frolic with nets, ice cream in hand.
The fireflies giggle, they play tag with me,
In broad daylight, how can this be?

Chasing dreams with a frozen treat,
While others find it quite a feat.
In this silly search for glowing orbs,
I trip on my laces, but my heart absorbs.

So I'll keep running, chasing the sun,
With laughter and pizza, it's all so fun.
For maybe in folly, the real treasure lays,
In the joy we find on silly, bright days.

The Allure of Misguided Journeys

I packed my bags to find my way,
A map turned upside down today.
With snacks and dreams, I hit the road,
Only to find a big toad on the load.

My friends warned me, but what did they know?
A journey's best with a little woe.
I followed a rainbow, but found a fence,
Do rainbows come with a sense of suspense?

Each detour leads to a new delight,
Like when I stumbled upon a chicken fight.
While searching for answers, I picked up a pie,
Now who knew pastries could make me fly?

So here I wander with crumbs on my shirt,
In pursuit of wisdom, but mostly dessert.
The road may twist, but I'll navigate,
With laughter and pie, oh, isn't it great?

Beneath the Weight of Unspoken Words

I've got secrets tucked under my hat,
Like why my cat seems so very fat.
With whispers trapped in a jammed-up jar,
I ponder if 'why' will take me far.

A mime once told me in silent chat,
His words were clearly so purr-fectly flat.
Each glance was a riddle, a puzzle to crack,
But all I could think was, 'Where's my snack?'

I hoard my thoughts like a squirrel with nuts,
Each day I wonder, "Why do I strut?"
In circles I walk, like a dance of dread,
If only my thoughts could come out instead.

So here I stand, with too much to say,
While my sentences play hide-and-seek today.
Perhaps out loud would set them free,
But then who would listen to my cat's decree?

Explorations in the Desert of Doubt

I trekked through sands of questioning haze,
Without a map, just lost in a daze.
My GPS said, 'Turn around and flee,',
But I swear, that cactus waved back at me!

With each step forward, I stumbled anew,
Digging for answers, but found only goo.
The breeze whispered tales of lost shoe lace,
Doubt twirls around me like a clown with a face.

Mirages dance just out of reach,
While tumbleweeds teach me how to breach.
Searching for wisdom in this barren land,
Ended up finding a sunburned hand.

Yet still I wander to see what's next,
In this silly mess, life's quite perplexed.
For in the desert, things shimmer and sway,
Perhaps that's a sign, or a missed buffet!

The Fever Dream of Contentment

In a world where socks get lost,
A treasure hunt for crumbs, at what cost?
Chasing comforts tucked in couch seams,
Dreaming big while bursting at the seams.

A chase for joy in cereal boxes,
Finding wisdom from wise old foxes.
Sipping tea from mugs that say 'Believe',
Buying bits of happiness like it's on sale this eve.

Chasing after clouds that seem so near,
While tripping over laughter, it's crystal clear.
The punchline's hidden under my dreams,
Adventures seems fine but nothing's as it seems.

In a maze of snacks, we boldly steer,
Hoping to find what's truly dear.
Who knew the quest was all for a slice?
Contentment made simple, but oh, what a price!

Lanterns Dimmed by Shadows.

With lanterns swaying, we roam the gloom,
Misguided souls set for certain doom.
Laughing at ghosts in fluorescent light,
Who knew the night held such funny fright?

Seeking answers in a basket of bread,
Chasing after thoughts, 'til we lose our head.
Searching for sense in silly routines,
Like counting all the jellybean means.

Clumsy joys wrapped in shadowy fuzz,
Fumbling for meaning, oh, just because.
Like hunting for gold in a pot of cheese,
Finding treasure where there's no time to squeeze.

Our lanterns flicker, lost in the fun,
Each shadow screams, "A race to be won!"
Yet here we stand, arms wide and grinning,
Life's crazy dance, oh what a beginning!

Whispers in Empty Corners

Whispers echo in corners so bare,
Searching for answers, but they aren't there.
Ticklish thoughts bounce like a ball,
Pretending to know when we actually stall.

The cat's tale holds secrets so grand,
Dreams of success scribbled in sand.
We flip through pages of old, dusty books,
Finding signs hidden in laughter's hooks.

In search of wisdom from a coffee shop,
Where wise folks teach you to dance and hop.
But all we learn is how to sip slow,
And laugh at ourselves, letting humor flow.

Those corners smile while we stumble and trip,
Sipping on nonsense, our wildest trip.
It's a comedy show in the dark of night,
Finding joy in whispers, what's wrong feels just right!

Shadows Chasing Light

Shadows frolic like they own the street,
Chasing light's fragrance, oh, how sweet.
With giggles and grins, they dance all around,
Fighting their fate, flipping upside down.

In pursuit of the sun, they play hide and seek,
Yet stumble in puddles that sound quite bleak.
They think they're clever, those wispy types,
Kicking up dust while checking their gripes.

Chasing the dawn with a wild, loud cheer,
But light simply giggles; it's never near.
Instead, it twirls in a whirl of delight,
Leaving shadows behind to chase through the night.

Yet when the laughter starts to fade,
And shadows grow weary of their charade,
They cuddle up close, resting in sight,
The chase was the fun, not the flicker of light!

Wandering in Shadows

In a world of neon signs, I roam,
Hoping to find the light that feels like home.
I trip over dreams like scattered toys,
And laugh at my chase, oh what a noise!

Signposts giggle, pointing the wrong way,
Leading me to cafes where cats come to play.
With every wrong turn, I snack on regret,
Adding sprinkles of joy, you wouldn't forget!

The compass spins wild like a cat on a spree,
As I dance through the night, clueless and free.
Each shadow a waltz, each laugh is a ray,
In this maze of missteps, I fake it each day.

So here's to the journey, whatever it holds,
With laughter our currency and chaos our gold.
We may be lost, but isn't it grand?
To stumble through life, with dessert in hand!

Illusions of Destiny

In a coffee shop, I sip my fate,
Stirring the cream like I'm on a date.
I swear I see signs written in foam,
But they lead me to places I can't call home.

Fortune cookies lie with a cunning grin,
Telling me wisdom just might be a sin.
I open one up, expecting a clue,
And it says, 'Buy more cookies, it's good for you!'

I thought I'd find meaning in yoga class,
But downward dog turned to a tumble and pass.
The universe whispers but I end up in knots,
With a voucher for saving on cream cheese shots.

Chasing the vision of what I should be,
I dance with illusions like leaves on the sea.
Perhaps I'll just settle for laughter and tea,
And toast to the fact that I'm just being me!

Echoes of a Thirsty Heart

At the bar with a drink, I ponder the scene,
While pondering choices of where I have been.
Every sip echoes like a riddle in air,
Do I need a map, or just a good chair?

I swipe left on plans that seem so grand,
While right swiping chaos is what I had planned.
Each chuckle I hear feels like a lost bet,
But I raise my glass; this isn't over yet!

My heart's compass spins like a carnival ride,
I chase down the laughter I keep deep inside.
Yet every round of shots feels heavy like art,
In the gallery of wishes, I print my own part.

So here's to the echoes that ring ever clear,
To the thirst for a path that feels warm and near.
Let's sip on the moments, as silly as they are,
Finding joy in confusion; just that's who we are!

Chasing Ghosts of Meaning

In haunted houses of thoughts I reside,
Seeking the specters with nowhere to hide.
Ghosts of ambition drift by in a haze,
I chase them in circles, caught in a daze.

I ask a wise owl; he just hoots in reply,
Scratches his head as I question the sky.
Each riddle he shares is like bubbles of air,
Floating away while I sit in despair.

I take to the streets with a map full of holes,
Playing hide and seek with my whimsical goals.
As the echoes of laughter chase shadows around,
I find that the jokes are the treasure I've found!

So here's to the phantoms we chase through the night,
Waving goodbye as we stumble in light.
In the quest for the meaning, let's make it a game,
For the laughter of living is never the same!

Breadcrumbs to Nowhere

I followed crumbs to the bakery,
Hoping for joy, but found a cake.
The frosting promised a sweet escape,
But all I got was a bellyache.

I searched for peace in the dog park,
Thought I'd find Zen in a playful bark.
Yet each pup tangled my shoelaces tight,
And I tripped in chaos, what a sight!

I sought deep meaning in a fortune cookie,
Expecting wisdom, perhaps a rookie.
But all it said was 'Try the lo mein',
Guess I'll eat noodles and dance in the rain.

I ventured out to find my groove,
Thought a yoga class would make me move.
But there's too much stretching, it's quite absurd,
Now I'm just a pretzel with a shoulder herd.

Wanderlust in the Wrong Direction

I packed my bags for a grand escape,
Heading east for a change of shape.
But ended up lost in a farmyard place,
Chased by chickens, what a weird race!

I boarded a train to a new hot spot,
Imagined vistas, but it's all for naught.
The only views were the passing trees,
And the dude next to me, snoring with ease.

I set out to hike in the great outdoors,
Dreaming of mountains and open doors.
But every trail led me back to town,
Fighting my GPS like a clown.

I took a ride in a tippy canoe,
Thought I'd find waves and a stunning view.
But we just spun in a circle by chance,
Now I'm landlocked at the lake doing a dance.

In Quest of Forgotten Truths

I rummaged through the attic of old,
Hoping for knowledge that had been sold.
Instead, I found socks from the eighties,
Fuzzy and bright, oh how it debates me!

I looked for wisdom in a dusty book,
Thought the universe would give me a look.
But it was just recipes, pages so yellow,
Now I'm baking pies with a quirkier hello.

I asked the wise owl sitting nearby,
His hoots were riddles, made me sigh.
In search for answers, I got a laugh,
Turns out he loves his cozy bath!

I searched for truth under the old oak tree,
Hoping for clarity, maybe a decree.
But found a squirrel with nuts to hoard,
Claiming he's king of the backyard horde.

Fragments of a Faded Compass

My compass pointed toward the sea,
But all I found was a stinging bee.
I chased it down with a silly sprint,
Ended up lost near a barbecue pit.

I tried to navigate through city streets,
Hoping for answers, maybe some treats.
But every turn just brought more cars,
Now I'm praying to those twinkling stars.

In pursuit of wisdom, I sought the sage,
Thought he'd bestow me with every page.
Instead, he told me to dance with glee,
Now I'm twirling like a tipsy bee!

I asked my phone for directions clear,
It led me to the nearest fast-food sphere.
With fries in hand, I pondered my fate,
Maybe lost is just an appetizer plate!

Compass of the Weary Traveler

With a map that points to ice cream shops,
He wanders through the town and plops.
His compass spins like a child's toy,
But where's the treasure? Oh look, a buoy!

The signs say 'left' but he goes right,
In search of gold, he finds a kite.
His compass says 'north' while he sips tea,
Laughing on the park bench, feeling so free.

A pirate once, or so he thought,
But now he just likes pastries a lot.
He'll never be rich, but at least he's fed,
Chasing dreams with crumbs instead.

So here's to those trips that lead us astray,
Where joy can be found in small bites of play.
His compass might fail, the map's a joke,
Yet in every flub, a smile strokes.

Serendipity in Unexpected Places

In laundromats where socks disappear,
He finds a fortune cookie, oh dear!
The message inside? Just laundry tips,
But with a twist, it leads to flips.

A balloon found on a busy street,
Leads him to find a dancing feet.
He tripped on fate, but hey, what's this?
A hula hoop? His moments of bliss.

While searching for wisdom in a book,
He stumbles and spills, oh what a rook!
The pages flutter, laughter ensues,
Inquirers gather, spreading good news.

Sometimes the gold is in silly gaffes,
Turning troubles to merriment laughs.
He may not know just where to look,
But serendipity is quite the hook.

Fading Footsteps in the Sand

He strolls along the beach, feeling grand,
But lose his flip-flops? So unplanned!
With every step, a squishy embrace,
As he laughs at his sand-covered face.

Chasing seagulls, they lead him astray,
What was once clear has now turned gray.
Footprints fading like last night's toast,
Where's the lighthouse? Now that's a roast!

He thought he'd discover the elusive map,
But all he found was a hand-knit cap.
Wind carries laughter, waves chant along,
While he hums absently a mismatched song.

Yet in the chaos, joy finds its scope,
Each misstep a pint of hope.
Fading footprints, but oh what fun!
In the dance of the waves, he's never done.

Hopes Tethered to a Wandering Heart

His heart's a kite stuck high in a tree,
Dreaming of places where he can be free.
He sets out with dreams on a rattly bike,
But ends up at a dog park, oh what a hike!

Pursuing signs that lead nowhere fast,
With hopes that flutter, but none held fast.
He befriends a dachshund, in search of clues,
Together they ponder, and share their views.

With each wrong turn, a laugh in the air,
His compass spins, but he doesn't care.
Tethered to joy, like string to a spool,
In life's grand circus, he's nobody's fool.

So raise a glass to hearts that roam high,
Finding magic in moments as they fly by.
Unraveled hopes, yet oh what a chart,
In the laugh of a friend, he finds his heart.

Windblown Words and Unspoken Dreams

In the park I lost my hat,
Chasing thoughts like a playful cat.
Every breeze whispers a clue,
But I trip over dreams, who knew?

Birds chirp gossip from the trees,
While I misread the flying bees.
Laughter bubbles in my chest,
They say my quest is quite the jest.

Clouds float by, what do they hold?
Maybe secrets, or stories untold.
But I'm stuck, like glue on a chair,
Trying to dance like I just don't care.

In this wild and windy show,
I wander where the lost hats go.
A purpose here, a giggle there,
Turns out I'm just a breath of air.

The Allure of Illusive Horizons

Chasing sunsets that run away,
Like my socks on laundry day.
Everyone's off to find their way,
While I'm stuck munching on hay.

The horizon winks, a sultry tease,
Drawing wanderers to their knees.
I stumble in a dazzling trance,
But trip on rainbows, miss the chance.

"Who am I?" the seagulls cry,
As I wave them off with a pie.
They don't care where I will land,
Still, I'm waiting for someone grand.

Through tangled paths of dreams untold,
I chase a tale that's growing old.
But laughter echoes in my head,
As I wander on, half alive, half dead.

Echoes in the Canyons of Time

Time giggles as it slips away,
Like a toddler in a game of play.
I shout to shadows, "Hey, come stay!"
But they prefer to dance and sway.

Rocks hum tunes of long-lost years,
While I juggle my hopes and fears.
"Let's find meaning," I declare loud,
But all I find is a playful cloud.

Footsteps echo in empty halls,
I slip and slide, oh how it sprawls.
Past lives whisper with sly delight,
As I fumble through my starry night.

In this grand and funny show,
Time strolls fast while I go slow.
I'm left to ponder, laugh, and scheme,
In the canyon of a silly dream.

A Pilgrim's Paradox

With compass spinning, I roam wide,
A pilgrim lost, not one to hide.
On treks of thought, I stomp and shout,
But wander off, without a doubt.

The road is paved with great advice,
Yet I trade wisdom for a slice.
A cupcake calls, "Forget the way,
Come find the fun, just here, hooray!"

In ancient books, I seek the truth,
While munching on my gummy tooth.
The sages glare, "Get back in line!"
But I'm busy tasting sour wine.

So here I am, a merry mess,
Chasing dreams in a funny dress.
In this paradox of laugh and sigh,
I'll find my way, or at least, I'll try.

Horizons Painted in Light and Shadow

Chasing dreams on a sunny day,
I tripped on my shoelaces, what can I say?
Found a map that led to a cheese shop,
Now I'm lost in fondue—oh, please don't stop!

Cloud gazing while munching on stale bread,
Hoping for wisdom, but landed instead,
In a field of flowers that whispered my name,
But all I got was a bad case of fame.

Each sunset radiates a funny tale,
Like missing the bus and setting sail.
In laughter, I find that joy stitches,
All my quirks and my little glitches.

So dance on the waves of this vast unknown,
As I juggle my dreams like a clown with a bone.
Each horizon beckons with light and shade,
But the fun is in the mess that I've made.

Drifting Amidst the Dunes

Sandy feet tell stories of tracks gone awry,
I tried to walk straight, but oh, how I'd fly!
Chasing mirages of camels with hats,
Turns out they're just goats—fancy that!

Wandering through dunes with a map upside down,
Found a party of cacti, in their prickly gown.
They danced like the pros in a shindig gone wild,
And I joined in, feeling like a child.

With each twist and turn, I laughed out loud,
Confetti of sand in my hair like a shroud.
The stars seem to giggle as I lose my way,
But hey, it's a party—come what may!

Drifting through life with my snacks in tow,
Or was that a sandwich? I'm losing the flow.
Embracing the chaos, I savored my plight,
In this buffet of blunders, I found pure light.

The Sound of Silence in Wilderness

In the quiet woods, my thoughts dance and sway,
Listening to leaves play hide-and-seek all day.
I thought I'd find answers in whispers or breeze,
But the squirrels just chattered—oh, what a tease!

I perched on a rock with a cup full of stew,
Pretending to meditate, but lost in my view.
A raccoon appeared, with mischief in mind,
And showed me that wisdom is utterly blind.

The trees stood like giants, with secrets to tell,
But their bark was so rough, they forgot how to yell.
I talked to a fox, who seemed rather wise,
But all he did was munch on some fries.

So now I sit sipping on nature's finest brew,
Wondering if stillness will lead me to you.
In silence I laugh at my grand, silly quest,
For the wilderness whispers that chaos is best.

Lessons from Wandering Souls

A hiker once trod where no path was found,
Thought he'd save time but just spun around.
He claimed that adventure was nobler than gold,
Yet slipped in a puddle—oh, if truth be told!

With a compass of chocolate and a map drawn in crumbs,

He set off with zeal, but forgot about plums.
Every step a drama, a near-miss with fate,
His laughter was clear, as he learned to relate.

The lessons he gathered like shells on the shore,
Each one a reminder that chaos can soar.
He found that the journey's what matters and gleams,
Even when life's a circus bursting at the seams.

So he danced through the mishaps with joy on display,
Wandering souls teach us to laugh anyway.
In the heart of the madness, he finally saw,
That purpose is laughter, not just some grand law.

Diverging Paths and Lonesome Roads

A hamster wheel spins, round and round,
I seek the lost socks I never found.
Chasing the ice cream truck, oh what a treat,
I end up lost in my own two feet.

Footprints in sand, which way did I go?
Following the cat, but wow, he's slow!
Maps in my pocket, they're all upside down,
Waving to strangers while we both frown.

Searching for treasure in the neighbor's yard,
Life's a week-long vacation that's really quite hard.
Jumping at junebugs, thinking they fly,
I should have taken a nap, oh me, oh my!

The road leads to coffee, it brightens my day,
But chocolate and chips have come out to play.
In this silly journey, I chuckle and grin,
Just a little lost, but I'm still all in.

A Mosaic of Misguided Journeys

Once I followed a squirrel, thought he'd know more,
He darted away, left me feeling sore.
Maps made of spaghetti, tangled and twirled,
My dreams dashed by noodles, oh what a world!

I bought a GPS, said 'Recalculating' twice,
Maybe I should try pizza, now that sounds nice!
Searching for gold, ended up with a rock,
A shiny one, at least, and a peculiar clock.

My compass spun wild, chasing illusions grand,
I waved at the moon, just to take a stand.
On rooftops I danced, thinking I'd fly,
Fell over a trash can, oh me, oh my!

Maps and directions, they just make me flip,
Navigating life's like a reality trip.
But amidst all the blunders, a lesson unfolds,
Laughter and giggles, they're worth more than gold.

Hearts Adrift in Shallow Waters

Once cast my line in the fountain of dreams,
Caught a rubber duck, or so it seems.
I splashed around hoping for fortune and fame,
But all I got was a soggy old game.

Floating like paper on a pond gone dry,
Searching for answers while ducks fly by.
Found a message in a bottle, just a cork,
Maybe I'll start a new trend—like a stork!

With life jackets made of marshmallows and fluff,
Each wave carries laughter, and that's quite enough.
I donned a pirate hat, set sail on a chair,
Treasure map leading to… where? Who knows where?

Adrift in the shallow, I smiled with glee,
For the best kind of treasure is just being me.
In puddles and ripples, I find joy anew,
Here's to whimsical journeys, and a duck or two!

Chasing Shadows Under the Moon

Under the moonlight, I thought I could dance,
But tripped on my own feet—oh, what a chance!
Shadows are tricky, they play hide and seek,
Whispering secrets that make me feel weak.

I chased my own shadow, thought it was fate,
But it turned into darkness—talk about late!
Puppies all barking, the laughter ignites,
Wishing on stars that flee from my sights.

Old shoes on the porch, I'm lost in the night,
Trying to figure what's wrong and what's right.
Do shadows hold wisdom or just silly games?
Guess I'll head home—this laughter still claims!

With moonbeams and giggles, I banish my gloom,
In the chase of my shadow, I dance in the room.
For laughter unravels, no maps or big plans,
Just spinning in circles, as life understands.

Broken Bottles

I once found wisdom in a bottle,
But it turned out to be just a throttle.
Pouring dreams on a party floor,
Now I laugh 'till I can't anymore.

I asked a cork for life advice,
It popped and fizzed, oh what a surprise.
With glass all shattered, humor did crack,
Who knew life's lessons came with a whack?

I sought my fortune in broken shards,
Glimmers of truth turned into marque cards.
Each step a stumble, each laugh a night,
Finding myself in the most chaotic light.

Now I toast to the chaos I've borne,
In the mess of my life, I've laughed 'til I'm worn.
For every bottle that ends in the sea,
There's a lesson I learned, oh to be free!

Unwritten Letters

I penned my dreams with a broken pen,
But the ink ran dry, back to square again.
With envelopes empty and stamps unstuck,
I laughed and thought, 'Ah, what good luck!'

Each letter I wrote went missing in space,
As if they sensed my awkward grace.
I tried to send one to the moon,
But all I got back was a goofy tune.

In hopes of guidance, I turned to a squirrel,
He just chattered; oh what a whirl!
Yet in this chaos, humor sprouts,
As I ponder my thoughts in doodled routes.

So here's to quests with no defined end,
Like scribbled notes to an unseen friend.
In each unwritten verse, I find delight,
Laughing at life with all of my might!

Rewrites in the Book of Life

I tried to draft my destiny's script,
But every chapter just seemed to slip.
With pencil in hand, I scribbled it wrong,
Yet somehow, the errors felt like a song.

My life's a novel with pages out of place,
Filled with typos in a chaotic race.
Each rewrite led to a hilarious twist,
Who knew that failure could come with a twist?

I read a book on how to be wise,
But the pages were stuck; oh what a surprise.
So I flipped it upside down, just for a laugh,
And found my fortune on the wrong side of the graph.

In laughter, I learned that it's all just a game,
With plots and subplots that are never the same.
So I'll keep on rewriting, and maybe one day,
I'll find my own style in a quirky ballet!

Colliding Stars

Two stars collided in a cosmic dance,
They spun and twirled, caught in a trance.
I thought they'd find purpose in their blaze,
Instead, they just giggled in a stellar haze.

I wished on a shooting star one night,
But all it did was give me a fright.
It veered off course, like it lost its way,
Now I laugh at the chaos in the Milky Way.

I sought to align in the celestial sphere,
Chasing the glow, but all I felt was sheer.
The universe whispered, 'Don't take it too hard,
Even stars need a break in the cosmic yard.'

So here's to the blunders that fill up the sky,
Cosmic hiccups that make me sigh.
With each laugh, I float like a comet's tail,
Finding joy in the stardust of life's wild trail!

Unmet Wishes

I tossed a dime in a fountain of dreams,
But it splashed back like it burst at the seams.
I wished for wisdom, but it came with a grin,
Turns out the fish were just here for their din.

Each wish I made felt like a game,
Stringing along with the same old name.
I wished for fortune and found a sock,
Laughed so hard, I could hardly walk.

A fairy showed up with a twinkle and laugh,
She asked if I'd like a free autograph.
I said, 'Sure, if you're giving it out,'
But she vanished in giggles, and I felt the doubt.

Yet in unmet wishes, I found my own cheer,
Like rain on a picnic; I'll bid it all dear.
For life's to be enjoyed, not taken with fright,
And in every mishap, I'll find pure delight!

The Veil of Distraction

I tried to focus on a grand ambition,
But Netflix whispered, 'Override your mission.'
With every click, my goals drifted away,
In a land of reruns, I chose to play.

My mind's a circus, filled with shiny things,
Like cats on treadmills and dogs with wings.
I chased a dream but got caught in a meme,
Now I chuckle at life's most whimsical scheme.

I asked for clarity, but got funny cat pics,
Reality blurred as I fell for the tricks.
Oh, what a journey through digital lands,
With laughter around me, I finally stand.

In the veil of distraction, I found some glee,
Every sidestep led to a new recipe.
So here's to the chaos, let it all sway,
For in distractions, I find a quirky way!

www.ingramcontent.com/pod-product-compliance
Lightning Source LLC
Chambersburg PA
CBHW051658160426
43209CB00004B/942